BATTLE FOR ANOTHER LEVEL

How God Can Transform Loss and Warfare
Into Deeper Intimacy

PAULA MARIE STEWART

BATTLE FOR ANOTHER LEVEL. Copyright © 2025. Paula Marie Stewart. All Rights Reserved.

Printed in the United States of America.

No portion of this book may be reproduced, stored in a retrieval system, or transmitted in any form or by any means, except for brief quotations in printed reviews, without the prior written permission of DayeLight Publishers or Paula Marie Stewart.

ISBN: 978-1-966723-32-5 (paperback)

Scripture quotations marked (NIV) are taken from the Holy Bible, New International Version®, NIV®. Copyright © 1973, 1978, 1984 by Biblica, Inc.™ Used by permission of Zondervan. All rights reserved worldwide.

ACKNOWLEDGEMENTS

Thanks to my Lord and Saviour, Jesus Christ, who has been my Lawyer, Battle Axe, Shield, Protector, and so much more.

Thanks to my family, my pastor, and his wife for their prayerful support and words of encouragement.

To my case-assigned intercessor, God will repay you for being a faithful and fearless servant.

To my network of intercessors, many thanks for the countless prayers. One shall chase a thousand and two will put ten thousand to flight; you all were much more than two.

To my church family, thank you all so much for being there in your own special ways.

TABLE OF CONTENTS

Acknowledgements iii
Introduction 7
The Beginning 9
Chapter 2 13
Chapter 3 17
Chapter 4 23
Chapter 5 35
Chapter 6 41
Chapter 7 55
Chapter 8 61
Chapter 9 63
Chapter 10 67
Chapter 11 73
Chapter 12 75
About the Author 81

INTRODUCTION

This book is my testimony of a specific period of my life, from 2021 to 2025. It outlines the challenges I faced: sicknesses, deaths, deceptions, witchcraft, but God's grace and mercy brought me through and enabled me to pursue, overcome, and recover; hence, possess my possession.

God is intentional and desires to get His glory at all times, so when He said, *"Write this book because others need to know,"* I had to obey. After all, it was obedience that allowed me to experience victory.

This book will help you understand that God can literally take you through battles once you are willing to listen and trust Him.

You will learn that God wants us to be His warriors and to continually progress from one level to the next.

I know this book will be a blessing to its readers. May God continue to bless you all.

THE BEGINNING

This chapter of my life started in 2021 during the COVID-19 pandemic. COVID-19 is a disease caused by the coronavirus. It was a period of great uncertainty, anxiety, and fear. In early September 2021, COVID-19 entered our home.

My mom and I had a very close relationship; we understood each other more than my other siblings did. She had health challenges such as diabetes, high blood pressure, and severe back pain. She also had surgery on her right wrist, which prevented her from tightly grasping things, and that made her frustrated. I lived with her, so I became her right hand and supported her as much as I could.

My mom often verbalized that she wanted to leave this world because of the pain she felt, and I always rebuked such thoughts. One day, as I watched her sleep peacefully, the thought came to me: *"This is what she would look like if she should pass."* I rebuked the thought.

I remembered the Lord gave me the song "Goodness of God" by CeCe Winans. At the time, I did not know the name of the singer or the lyrics, and it did not mean much to me. However, later it became my 'go-to' song.

Unfortunately, my mom contracted COVID-19. She did not want to go to the doctor for confirmation, but all the symptoms were present. We used most of the home remedies that were recommended, including various teas, drinks, and steaming. After not seeing any improvement, and other family members started exhibiting similar symptoms, I encouraged her to go to the doctor.

She reluctantly agreed. She was given medication and sent to do the COVID test. The test site was full to capacity. She became restless, so we took her home, and she began taking the medication. We stayed up with her the entire night, comforted and cared for her.

She refused to eat because COVID had affected her sense of taste, hence the food was not palatable to her. After much begging and pleading, she was given some soup. About two days later, and still no improvement, we took her to the hospital. The doctor informed us that her blood pressure and blood sugar levels were high. He recommended that she do the COVID test at the hospital, which she did, and the result was positive. She received medication for her high blood pressure and diabetes, and was released because she did not display any respiratory difficulties. My mom told the doctor that she was dying. Both the doctor and I replied, *"We speak life."*

Before we could leave the hospital, she started having problems breathing, so she was given oxygen. Upon the doctor's return, he was surprised to find that she was still there. He said, *"What are you doing on oxygen? Don't you want to go home?"* She was too weak and did not answer. I spent the night with her there. I left in the morning to get some supplies she needed. On my return, I was informed that no visitors were allowed on the wards. All items were to be left at the reception area, and they would be delivered to the patients.

The Lord had prepared me for this. He told me what to do to ensure I got back on the ward.

My mom had accepted the Lord as her personal saviour before she was admitted to the hospital. The Lord told Sandy, a family friend, to tell her that He was waiting for her to accept Him as her Lord and Saviour. I was elated that she had accepted Christ because I had always encouraged her to surrender her life to Christ totally. She regularly attended church with me on Sundays, but was not committed to the faith.

By obeying the Lord's instructions, I got on the ward. My mother was tired and wanted the oxygen mask taken off. I asked her if she didn't want to go home with us, because my stepfather was waiting outside, but she didn't respond. I gave her a bath and changed her bedding. She said, *"I want to go home; there is too much noise here."* Then I noticed that her breathing was shallow. She turned her head away from me, placed her hand on my shoulder, and took her last breath.

CHAPTER 2

I stood there looking at her, and the Lord said to me in my spirit, *"Don't allow anyone to tell you that COVID took her life because I am the one who called her home."*

I was shocked, but I felt a sense of great peace. A patient nearby who witnessed the incident advised me to call the doctor.

The doctor rubbed her chest and beckoned me to follow him; then he disclosed what I already knew. I went back and looked at her. The same patient said, *"You need to cry or you will faint."*

I turned my attention to the body of my mom and said, *"You left me."* Then the tears flowed, and I placed my head on her chest. The nurse advised me not to put my head on her, but I didn't care. The hospital orderly took her body to the morgue. I just stood there and watched with tears streaming down my face. Even now, as I write, the tears are coming.

I then had to go and tell her husband she had passed. This was not easy, and as expected, he broke down, but somehow he managed to drive us home. It was now time to break the news to my other siblings. As we entered our home, my sister knew. We hugged and cried. I also informed my church family, who were praying for me, as well as my other family members and neighbors.

The Lord was indeed with me. I did not feel the grief I should have because He knew what was to come. It was hard for me; I questioned the Lord because I had pleaded with Him to give her more time.

I was supported and encouraged by my pastor, his wife, my church family, the gentleman I was dating, and my close friends. What also helped me to deal with the loss was that I knew she was pain-free; no more suffering. The Lord comforted me, and I prayed that others would experience the same comfort He had given me.

We took the COVID test that the hospital had requested. Everyone in the household tested positive, except me. The miracle-working God, in whom I trust, was in the midst of everything. He protected me, not because I am special but for His glory. I am not here to explain it, and I will not try to, but He does what He sees fit.

CHAPTER 3

I got married two months after my mom passed. I was 50 years old. I prayed for years, but nothing happened. I even got engaged at one point, but that story is for another time. At one point, I engaged in introspection and realized that the fault lay with me.

The Lord had sent people into my life, but I found faults, not understanding that God is in charge and knows what is best for me. I allowed the enemy to rob me of many things, but I did not realise until much later. I was upset with God. Others were getting married, and He wasn't making it happen for me. I decided to stop living a life that pleased God and started living my life my way.

How foolish of me! You cannot force the hand of God, and if you fight God, you will not win. At one point, I almost backslid. I received a call from Sister Ann, one of the prayer warriors at my church. She said the Lord told her that I was backsliding and that no one was aware. Consumed with guilt, I did not respond; however, she prayed for me. With that revelation, I decided to set aside my longing for marriage. I prayed regularly and fasted once per week to rebuild my relationship with the Lord.

One day, Sister Ann came and told me that she had dreamed that I was preparing to get married. I thought it was interesting. I was excited to hear this. One day, I felt lonely, and I told the Lord that I would like a male friend, not for marriage, but for companionship. I found that males communicated more objectively and provided different perspectives than females did.

One night, I had a dream in which I was talking to a man in a way that suggested he was my husband. I had the dream three consecutive nights. When I awoke, I told the Lord, *"Please give me the heart to accept whomever You will send."*

A dear friend, whom I refer to as my second mom, had returned from overseas. One day, she said that she was told to show me a photograph. Her statement piqued my interest. She handed me a photograph of a gentleman who was much older than I was; he had long hair and a beard. She asked me what I thought. I responded, *"Which hippy is this you're showing me?"* Oh, I did not mention that he is of Asian descent. She was a bit upset and said, *"He can cut his hair."* I was not impressed. He was not my type.

At home, later that afternoon, I thought of the man in the photograph. My assessment of him was that he is not of my race; he is old and has a lot of hair. Then the Lord spoke into my spirit, *"Didn't you say you wanted a male to talk to? Why not speak to him? He wants someone to talk to as well."* The next day, I told my second mom to ask him to call me, and she did.

He was very pleasant, and our conversation flowed smoothly. He said I was too young, and of course, I told him he was too old, so we decided to be friends. Our friendship blossomed. He was a Christian, so we had nightly devotion. We talked about the Lord and life in general. We built an authentic friendship. With great ease, we discussed topics that some people would be embarrassed to talk about, such as regular bowel movements.

He was caring, respectful, calm, warm, thoughtful, kind, understanding, patient, peaceful, loving, family-oriented, gentle, and loved to laugh. We had a lot of FaceTime, even while I was on the road. My mom knew of him, and they spoke on the phone.

One day, he said, *"Why don't we inquire of the Lord if we should take this relationship to the next level?"* This was like six months of friendship, so we sought the Lord. We each asked persons we trusted, and who had a strong prayer life, to intercede on our behalf.

The answer came back, indicating that God favoured the relationship to move to the next level. From that point, he referred to himself as my Boaz. He was so funny, and interestingly, the Lord had given me the book of Ruth to study a few months earlier.

He planned to visit Jamaica a few times, but would change his mind. The number of COVID cases had declined, my mother had passed, so he wanted to attend her funeral to support me. I told him to wait for a further decline in the COVID cases.

He, along with my church family, provided a lot of emotional support during my mom's illness and passing. He wanted to come, but I discouraged him as the rest of my household had tested positive for COVID.

We discussed marriage and examined rings, but we did not set a date. He wanted to see me in person before we made the final plans.

At the beginning of November, he made plans to visit Jamaica; then, two days before his arrival, he cancelled. I was very upset. Remember, I was grieving, and for him to disappoint me, I thought he was inconsiderate. I prayed and shared my frustrations with Sandy, who is an intercessor. She told me, *"Don't you see that the enemy doesn't want you to get married."*

I spent three days in prayer and fasting regarding the matter. On the third day, he called to say he was coming later that month. He sent me phone numbers for his daughter, sister, and brother. His sister did not want us to get married. The Lord told me not to tell anyone of his coming until he arrived. I obeyed the Holy Spirit.

He arrived on the 21st of November 2021. I picked him up at the Knutsford's Express bus terminal, and a few hours later, he proposed. I was very excited; I called Sandy and told her. She said, *"Have the ring blessed and do not wear it because you know that the enemy does not want you to get married."* As excited as I was, I did not wear the ring.

We got married at my home on November 28th, supported by my family and a few close friends. None of his family members attended, including his sister, who lives in Jamaica. She did not want to be a part of it. I spoke to his daughter, who did not express any opposition to the marriage. Her concern was his happiness. She wanted to know that he was happy. We were both very happy.

The following day, we went on a week-long honeymoon. It was wonderful.

On our return from the honeymoon, he said, *"I want you to have a home and be happy because I am your Boaz."* He also said, *"I'm going back before Christmas because I have another appointment with the cardiologist."* He also wanted to return home to attend to some business and start the U.S. spousal visa application process. I was not happy that he was leaving so soon, but I agreed with his decision and prayed about the doctor's appointment.

He returned home on December 9th. We spoke frequently and made plans regarding his return to Jamaica.

CHAPTER 4

His appointment was set for December 22nd. He told me that it was a simple procedure that would require him to stay in the hospital overnight, and he should be fully recovered in three days. After the procedure, his blood pressure went up, so he spent an extra night. He was then released, but he experienced frequent bouts of hiccups, an upset stomach, and felt lethargic. I asked him if it was possible to get a friend to stay with him. I suggested that he take some over-the-counter medication to relieve the upset stomach. Unfortunately, the medication did not work, so he decided to go to another hospital. I really did not want him to go, but since he was the one experiencing the discomfort, I reluctantly encouraged him to go.

We kept communicating. He told me that the hospital found out that he had COVID; however, when he left Jamaica, he was COVID-negative. I assumed he contracted it while in the first hospital. I was extremely concerned and very upset that the hospital did not perform a COVID test before the procedure. He received a supply of oxygen, and he said that he felt much better. I breathe a sigh of relief. He said he had eaten; however, he still felt weak and was still experiencing hiccups. On the 29th of December, he was placed on a ventilator as his condition had gotten more serious. I was terrified, but his nurse assured me that it would only be for a little while. I then realized that he had not told me the seriousness of his illness.

On the 31st of December, I requested prayer for him from a women's group that I was a part of and from my pastor. Seeing that he was on the ventilator, we were unable to communicate. I had no one to call to find out how he was doing, so I searched for his daughter's number, which I found. While I was at a family event in St. Ann, I called her. She asked how I got her number. I told her she did not seem pleased about receiving my call.

However, she updated me on his condition and said that he was not looking too good. I cried the whole way home from the family event. I called Sandy, told her about his condition, and that I would not be attending church in the morning. She convinced me that I should go to the house of the Lord for strength and encouragement.

I went to church, and while I was there, the Spirit of the Lord spoke to me and said, *"Go and testify about what is happening, because this situation is much bigger than you."* I did not want to do it, but I really could not carry the burden alone, so I complied. I shared with the entire congregation, as well as the online viewers, what I was going through and that I craved their prayers.

His daughter did not use WhatsApp, which made calling expensive for me. I found the hospital's number on Google and called, but no one picked up; all I heard were recordings. Some of his friends, who lived in Canada, sent credit to my phone so I could call the hospital often. The recordings used up my credit; I got no information, and I was frustrated. I reached out to his daughter again, who stated that he was not looking as bad as the day before.

My husband's friends suggested that I ask the hospital for a letter to apply for an emergency visitor's visa. I asked his daughter to request the letter, which she did, and I received it on January 6th, 2022. I applied through a travel agency and got an appointment for an interview in two weeks.

Leading up to the day of the interview, I prayed, *"Lord, I don't know if this is Your will, but let Your will be done."* I attended the interview at the U.S. Embassy, and I was denied the visa.

Strangely, the denial did not devastate me. I had peace. I would later come to understand why God did not allow me to go. When I explained to people that, despite the letter from the hospital, I was still denied the visa, they were taken aback. I understand their reaction, but when God is in a situation, the results are not the usual or what is expected.

His daughter had downloaded WhatsApp, so I informed her of the outcome of my Embassy interview. She did not believe what she heard, so I sent her the evidence of the visa denial. I knew it was a challenge for her to go to the hospital every day or every other day. On the days she did not go, I called the hospital to check on him. By then, I understood how to get a call through to the ward. The nurses informed me about his condition. Whenever his daughter visited, I FaceTimed him; we sang hymns and choruses, and I read scriptures to him. I made jokes about both of us being members of the *"Can't Sing Choir."*

On one of the calls with his daughter, she allowed me to speak with his nurse, who informed me that the doctors said that his lungs were damaged. He needed a tracheotomy, and he needed to be in a hospice. I blurred out, *"That's a lie from the pit of hell."* The nurse was surprised, but I was not accepting that report. I was not in a position to make any medical decisions on his behalf because he had given power of attorney to his sister in Jamaica. Although we were married, it did not change automatically; he would have to revoke the power of attorney. I said, *"I'm not accepting that. I totally believe in God for a better report."* I asked the nurse, *"Do you believe in God?"* She said, *"Yes."* I told her to believe with me for a turnaround, and she said yes.

She handed the phone to his daughter, and she allowed me to see him. He had tubes all over. I prayed with him and recited Psalm 121, then ended the call.

When I got off the phone, I cried; I was inconsolable. Sometime later, his daughter called me to inquire how I was doing because she realised that I was hurting. She stated that she too was very concerned about his condition, and she was at his house to get some items to return to the hospital. I couldn't handle the conversation, so I ended the call.

I threw myself on the floor and cried uncontrollably. My body felt numb, and I was despondent. I called

Sandy and requested prayer. I cried until there were no more tears. I was still on the floor when the Lord said, *"Get up, have a bath, and eat."*

I did not want to, but it kept echoing in my head: *"Get up, have a bath, and eat."* So I did.

After I ate, I felt a little better. I thought that if I believed in God for a miracle, I should praise Him, so I praised Him. He gave me these scriptures:

> ***Matthew 7:8 - For everyone who asks receives; the one who seeks finds; and to the one who knocks, the door will be opened. (NIV).***
>
> ***Psalm 27:1-14 - The LORD is my light and my salvation—whom shall I fear? The LORD is the stronghold of my life—of whom shall I be afraid? When the wicked advance against me to devour me, it is my enemies and my foes who will stumble and fall. Though an army besiege me, my heart will not fear; though war break out against me, even then I will be confident. One thing I ask from the LORD, this only do I seek: that I may dwell in the house of the LORD all the days of my life, to gaze on the beauty of the***

LORD and to seek him in his temple. For in the day of trouble he will keep me safe in his dwelling; he will hide me in the shelter of his sacred tent and set me high upon a rock. Then my head will be exalted above the enemies who surround me; at his sacred tent I will sacrifice with shouts of joy; I will sing and make music to the LORD. Hear my voice when I call, LORD; be merciful to me and answer me. My heart says of you, "Seek his face!" Your face, LORD, I will seek. Do not hide your face from me, do not turn your servant away in anger; you have been my helper. Do not reject me or forsake me, God my Savior. Though my father and mother forsake me, the LORD will receive me. Teach me your way, LORD; lead me in a straight path because of my oppressors. Do not turn me over to the desire of my foes, for false witnesses rise up against me, spouting malicious accusations. I remain confident of this: I will see the goodness of the LORD in the land of the living. Wait for the LORD; be strong and take heart and wait for the LORD. (NIV).

Micah 2:1-3 - Woe to those who plan iniquity, to those who plot evil on their beds!

At morning's light they carry it out because it is in their power to do it. They covet fields and seize them, and houses, and take them. They defraud people of their homes; they rob them of their inheritance. Therefore, the LORD says: "I am planning a disaster against this people, from which you cannot save yourselves. You will no longer walk proudly, for it will be a time of calamity." (NIV).

The Lord said, *"It is you the devil wants to destroy and your testimony."* My dear friends, I honestly did not understand what the Lord was saying.

Sonia, another intercessor friend and neighbor, told me that God allowed the situation and I should maintain my confidence in Him. With that information, I fasted and prayed more fervently, waiting for my miracle.

A few days later, I called the hospital to check on him. The nurse told me that his oxygen supply had increased to 55% because his oxygen level kept fluctuating; however, the oxygen in his blood was at 95%. I felt a little more hopeful, although I did not fully comprehend what it meant medically. I asked the nurse if she knew the Lord as her personal Savior, and she responded, *"Yes."* I told her I was praying for her and the other hospital staff members. She thanked me, and our conversation ended.

I texted his daughter and visited Sonia. We discussed my situation. She said, *"Your testimony is going to be great."* I agreed with her. Just then, I received a text from his daughter, which stated that she was on the phone with his sister and they were planning his funeral because the hospital wanted permission to remove him from the ventilator. *The horror and shock!* I experienced an emotional overload. I pleaded with her not to go ahead with that plan. I knew his sister did not want to talk to me because she was not in agreement with our marriage. Hence, his daughter was the only person I communicated with. She said she would share my pleas with her aunt.

I was extremely upset; as soon as the call ended, I declared that only God's will must be done. Sonia agreed with me; I called all the people who supported me in prayer. They were all shocked by the situation and declared their intention to remain steadfast in prayer.

I fasted and prayed, and hoped that he would be healed and be able to share his testimony when he returned to Jamaica.

On January 13th, 2022, his daughter informed me by text message that she was on her way to the hospital. Upon her arrival, she reported that there were no changes in his condition. She made a video call, which allowed me to see him. I prayed with him and read the 23rd Psalm.

> *Psalm 23:1-6 - The LORD is my shepherd, I lack nothing. He makes me lie down in green pastures, he leads me beside quiet waters, He refreshes my soul. He guides me along the right paths for his name's sake. Even though I walk through the darkest valley, I will fear no evil, for you are with me; your rod and your staff, they comfort me. You prepare a table before me in the presence of my enemies. You anoint my head with oil; my cup overflows. Surely your goodness and love will follow me all the days of my life, and I will dwell in the house of the LORD forever. (NIV).*

For most of the night, I prayed and listened to the inspiring messages of Apostle Joshua Selman, whose teachings were sources of great strength, especially the one entitled 'Rules of Engagement.'

One night, I had many dreams; in one of them, I dreamed that my husband came back to Jamaica, and we were sewing together. I did not always understand some of the dreams, but most of the time they were accurate and came through. Later that morning, I checked on my husband, and his condition had deteriorated, but I kept the faith.

On January 15th, Sandy called and gave me a song she believed the Lord wanted me to listen to. It was Tobb Gaiberth's 'The Anthem/Resurrecting Power.' The song truly ministered to me. She said that something had broken. She also added that the Lord said, "It's rejoicing time."

I rejoiced more than I ever did. With that revelation, and then my aunt called to say she felt in her spirit that he would pull through, my faith increased significantly.

CHAPTER 5

On January 16th, I dreamt that I was in the washroom and my deceased mom was in the kitchen. There was a lizard, and it ran and jumped. I did not see where it went. I covered my mouth with my hand only to discover that the lizard was hanging onto my tooth. I pulled it from my tooth and squeezed it, while I repeated *"A dead you dead now."* I woke up feeling exhausted.

The dream was a serious one, but it showed that I had overcome the enemy. Indeed, Satan was working to destroy me, but God made me victorious.

On January 17th, I called the hospital and was told that he was COVID-free. Glory to God!

Although COVID was out of his system, his lungs were damaged, and his oxygen level was at 75%. His daughter called later in the day and said she would be visiting him, and the hospital was unable to get in touch with his sister. In my heart, I rejoiced, thanked Jesus, and whispered, *"Lord, have Your way. Do not allow them to take him off the ventilator until You are ready, God."*

On January 18th, I asked the nurse if there was a policy that he should be taken off the ventilator. She said that the decision was the patient's caregiver's to make, not the hospital's. Just as I thought: his daughter was lying to me. I asked the nurse how he was doing. She said I should ask his daughter.

What is this!

I felt anxious, nauseous, and angry.

Suddenly, I remembered a YouTube message I had listened to entitled ***"Your Destiny Requires Wilderness Season."*** The preacher said that whenever we face difficult situations, we often get upset with God and complain. We are unaware that God is preparing us to help others, and the experience will build our faith, trust, and character. The Lord sees things in us that will be a hindrance to our next level. We must confess those hindrances; some will remove themselves, and God will remove others. They have to go so that God can entrust us with our new assignment.

At a prayer meeting one morning, this scripture ministered to me:

Isaiah 30:18-31 - Yet the LORD longs to be gracious to you; therefore he will rise up to show you compassion. For the LORD is a God of justice. Blessed are all who wait for him! People of Zion, who live in Jerusalem, you will weep no more. How gracious he will be when you cry for help! As soon as he hears, he will answer you. Although the Lord gives you the bread of adversity and the water of affliction, your teachers will be hidden no more; with your own eyes you will see them. Whether you turn to the right or to the left, your ears will hear a voice behind you, saying, "This is the way; walk in it." Then you will desecrate your idols overlaid with silver and your images covered with gold; you will throw them away like a menstrual cloth and say to them, "Away with you!" He will also send you rain for the seed you sow in the ground, and the food that comes from the land will be rich and plentiful. In that day your cattle will graze in broad meadows. The oxen and donkeys that work the soil will eat fodder and mash, spread out with fork and shovel. In the day of great slaughter, when the towers fall, streams of water will flow on every high mountain and every lofty hill. The moon will shine like the sun, and the sunlight will be seven times brighter, like the light of seven full days, when the LORD binds up the bruises of his people and heals the wounds he inflicted. See, the Name of the LORD comes from afar, with burning anger and dense clouds of smoke; his lips are full of wrath, and his tongue is a consuming fire. His breath is like a rushing torrent, rising up to the neck. He shakes the nations in the sieve of destruction; He places in the jaws of the peoples a bit that leads them astray. And you will sing as on the night you celebrate a holy festival; your hearts will rejoice as when people playing pipes go up to the mountain of the LORD, to the Rock of Israel. The LORD will cause people to hear his majestic voice and will make them see his arm coming down with raging anger and consuming fire, with cloudburst, thunderstorm and hail. The voice of the LORD will shatter Assyria; with his rod he will strike them down. (NIV).

I cried out to the Lord, *"Oh my Lord, this is too much. I don't understand completely what You are saying. This is hard, Lord. Why? Please, help me!"*

I went to bed with my mind in a whirl, utterly confused, so I put my earpads in and listened to a sermon. I eventually fell asleep in the wee hours of the morning. I dreamt that my dearly beloved husband said he had to call me because he wanted to hear my voice, and he missed me. I said to him, *"You are off the oxygen, so be careful. Your throat is sore, so don't talk too much. I miss you, but hearing your voice makes me happy."* The dream felt so real that I woke up wondering if it was a dream or if it had really happened.

CHAPTER 6

On the morning of January 19th, I received a call from an old friend who knew my husband. First, let me explain how this friend came back into my life. She was a church sister who had migrated to the United States of America. My husband went to her place of employment to conduct business on my behalf. During the transaction, she told him that she was from Jamaica and the specific community in which she resided. He was so excited to ask me if I knew her, which I did, so she and I reconnected.

Now back to the reason she called. She began, *"Paula, I'm so sorry about your loss."*

"What!" I screamed.

She continued, *"I'm so sorry. I didn't know you were not aware that he passed last night. They took him off the ventilator, and he suffered a heart attack."*

"Jesus!" I shouted. I cried so hard, I don't remember to this day if I hung up or she did. The pain was unbearable, and there were many feelings I could not describe. Even as I write, recalling that conversation brought tears to my eyes.

The pain of the loss of my mom just a few months earlier was nothing compared to this. The Lord had prepared me emotionally and spiritually for my mom's passing because He knew I would soon have to deal with the passing of another loved one. The Lord knew that on my own, I could not handle the intensity of both deaths.

Jesus!

I cried the entire day. I called his daughter constantly without success, which made me feel even worse. I cried throughout the night into the following morning. I felt like my head was about to explode. The Lord spoke into my spirit, *"Paula, do you want to end up in the hospital? COVID is down there."* It did not matter to me because I had lost my mom and now my husband, the man whom I had come to love so much. I said to the Lord, *"Now I know why people don't serve You, and why they turn their backs on You. Why? What have I done to deserve this?"* He was silent. I cried some more. No one in my house could comfort me. I did not want to be comforted, speak to anyone, or see anyone.

Again, the Lord spoke, *"Do you want to end up in the hospital? Tie your head and get up. You have some molasses in the cupboard. Go drink some."* I just lay there. I had no tears left, but I was still crying. After a while, I said to the Lord, *"You want to kill me, go ahead, because I'm not going anywhere. I'm not going to suffer with You, and go suffer with Satan in hell. Kill me too."* He was silent. I had now tied my head, and after some time, I got up, went to the cupboard, and there was the molasses. I didn't even remember I had it because I usually drank it while my mom was alive. I thought it was finished. The moment I drank it and it entered my digestive system, I felt relaxed and fell asleep.

I felt a little better the following day, but I spent the whole day in my room. I thought about how my husband was just perfect for me; not that he was perfect, but there was no pretense in him. He truly cared for me and knew how to help me avoid being miserable. To reassure me of his commitment to me, he often told me, *"Paula, I want you to be happy. You're my darling wife, and I am your Boaz."*

My spirit was broken. We were a perfect fit for each other. I looked at his clothes and thought, *"How could this be? Even his clothes and shoes fit me. Jesus, help! Please take the pain."*

The Lord had wiped me out; the two people I knew I could depend on, and I knew truly loved me, were gone—just like that. I felt such great emptiness. *What was I going to do now?*

On January 29th, I continued to call his daughter, but as usual, there was no answer. The one person I hoped would give me some clarity did not answer my calls. I was confused, and doubts filled my mind.

A new day dawned, but the pains continued. I felt the need to get out of the house, so I walked to my brother's house, with tears streaming down my face. When I got there, my young niece and nephew, oblivious to the depth of my situation, spoke about their concerns, which caused some distractions from my pain.

I returned home and called his daughter again; still, there was no answer. I then remembered that he had given me the telephone number for his sister's place of employment. I called, and she answered. I knew it was her, but she denied it. Just before she hung up, there was a quiet laugh. Based on the information he had given me, the number was her private line; I knew it was her. Disappointed and confused, I asked, *"What next, Lord? I didn't kill him, so why must I suffer like this?"*

I received a great deal of support from people at my church and the women's group I was part of. They called and prayed with me. Fortunately for me, they did not ask many questions, which I really did not want, because honestly, I did not have the answers.

Later in the day, I received a call from a man who claimed to be a friend of my husband's family. Instinctively, I knew he had some connections to my husband's sister, who had pretended not to be the person who answered my call. He asked, *"Why are you calling the family?"*

Wow! What a question!

The man was my husband, regardless of the fact that she did not agree with the marriage.

I told him I had the right to know what had happened to my husband. He stated, *"How could you have gotten married to him without the family meeting and agreeing to the marriage?"*

I responded, *"It was all on her (his sister) because she did not want to meet me."*

He said, *"It was COVID time, and she could not meet with you."*

I replied, *"She did not even want to speak with me on the phone. By the way, do you realize that my husband is a grown man and the final decision regarding his life is his to make."* He agreed. I asked him if my husband had really passed, and he said yes. God strengthened me. I questioned him about how and when my husband passed. He indeed passed the day my friend called and gave her condolences. According to him, the rest of the family did not want him off the ventilator, but his sister said that my husband had a no resuscitation request, so she made the decision to take him off, and that was when he suffered the heart attack.

"Do you know when the funeral will be?" I asked. He did not know the details of the funeral arrangements; however, he knew that my husband's body would be cremated. He told me that my husband's daughter was dealing with the funeral arrangements.

He asked, *"Did you know that he wanted to be cremated?"*

I replied, *"Yes, I knew, and he had also made provision for the payment of his funeral."*

I asked him to please get the date of the funeral service from the daughter. He said he would try.

The Lord provided me with information. I heard it almost from the horse's mouth. I was surprised by my own reaction. *Where did this strength and peace come from?* Must be from the prayers of the saints. I felt a strange comfort knowing what had taken place. I chose to believe him. He said he was a friend of the family, but I knew he was no friend; he was the sister's son and my husband's favorite nephew. *How do I know?* He had called me on WhatsApp, and his photo appeared when I saved his number. My husband had sent me a photograph of him because he had gotten married and migrated to the USA. He had inquired of his uncle about the spousal visa application process.

A few days passed, and I heard nothing from him. I was anxious, so I called him, but there was no answer. I called my husband's friends, but they too heard nothing. I emailed his daughter and pleaded with her to provide some information about the funeral, but she did not respond.

I asked my brother, who lives in the USA, to check if the death had been registered. My brother reported that there was no death registered under that name. I thought maybe he was not dead and they were hiding him from me. *Wow, could they be so wicked?* I did not understand why his daughter was not communicating with me, as we had developed a mutual respect for each other. Well, that's what I thought.

It was now Sunday, so I attended church, and I was fasting to hear a response to my unanswered calls and texts. While I prayed, my niece came to mind, and the Lord spoke into my spirit, *"Go to her house and go around the house three times."*

I said to the Lord, *"I'm grieving, and I'm to go do what?"* Of course, He said nothing. When I arrived, my sister-in-law was outside washing.

She started a conversation with me, and the Lord spoke again, *"What did I send you here to do?"*

I thought to myself, *"People will think I'm working obeah."*

Anyway, I went around the house and prayed as I walked. My niece found it strange, so she called out to me, *"Auntie, how you don't greet me? You just going round the house?"* I raised my hand to her and kept going. I spoke in tongues (an unknown language) as I prayed. When I was finished, they asked me about what I had done, and I told them that I was just following God's instructions. Then I left.

It was now Thursday, and I still hadn't heard anything from my husband's relatives. I visited my niece only to be told that a gunman invaded one of their premises and persons were shot. My niece's mother explained how they tried to hide and how the shooter stared at her. The Lord said, *"The shooter did not see you."* God is the all-powerful one.

Let me pause to say that obedience is very critical in walking with the Lord. The devil's plan was to come and take my brother and his wife. Bear in mind, I lost my mom in September 2021, my husband on January 19th, 2022, and now this, in the same month of January, but God! Hallelujah! Thank You, Jesus! Had Satan's plans materialised, only God knows what would have become of me. Thank You, Lord, for loving me so, so much.

At the end of January, I was very depressed, and I sent a voicenote, in which I was crying, to ask his nephew for information about the funeral service. He called and said the cremation would take place that week, but he did not know of a funeral service. I was extremely frustrated.

I cried, *"God, what did I do to deserve this?"* My grief continued for the next few days. Then the thought came to me to call his friends in Canada. When I called, they were also seeking information about the cremation, but got nothing. I told his friend I needed closure. He said his sister-in-law, who lived in Miami, could get the death certificate if I sent her the required information. I was relieved to know that the possibility existed for me to put to rest the confusion and distress I was experiencing.

After a few days, his friend sent me a copy of the death certificate via WhatsApp. It was surreal; I kept looking at it and thinking, *"I cannot believe I'm seeing his name on this document."*

Jesus, this is it! He is no longer here! I'm not going to see him again; it's over. I cried, oh, how I cried.

After crying, I felt a sense of peace. I thanked God for the confirmation of his death, but then came the thought that the document could be fake. *Wow! Really?* So I requested that the original death certificate be sent to me. I waited with trepidation for its arrival. I called the friend, and he assured me it was sent. He confessed that he deliberately withheld a specific section of the death certificate from me. He promised to send a picture of it, so I wouldn't be caught off guard when the original arrived. The section I received required information about the deceased's surviving spouse. His daughter wrote that he had no surviving spouse.

Have you ever watched a cartoon with an angry bull with smoke coming through his nostrils and ears? That was me. I called his friend and asked why he withheld it from me. He said he was trying to protect me; he did not want me to fall into a deeper depression. I was mad at him, but kept it to myself. I hung up the phone and blasted the daughter and her aunt because they were in collusion.

Eventually, I calmed down, and the Lord spoke to me. *"They're not aware that you have a copy of the death certificate, and worst, you also have the daughter's address on the death certificate."* The Lord led me to read Esther 3:6, where Haman plotted to kill Mordecai and to destroy the rest of the Jews, and Esther declared a fast.

There was no doubt that the Lord was giving me instructions, because the enemy is real. These people were plotting against me to my detriment.

The Lord also gave me **Psalm 53,** and said I should focus on verses **5-6:**

Psalm 53:1-4 - The fool says in his heart, "There is no God." They are corrupt, and their ways are vile; there is no one who does good. God looks down from heaven on all mankind to see if there are any who understand, any who seek God. Everyone has turned away, all have become corrupt; there is no one who does good, not even one. Do all these evildoers know nothing? They devour my people as though eating bread; they never call on God." (NIV).

Psalm 53:5-6 - But there they are, overwhelmed with dread, where there was nothing to dread. God scattered the bones of those who attacked you; you put them to shame, for God despised them. Oh, that salvation for Israel would come out of Zion! When God restores his people, let Jacob rejoice and Israel be glad! (NIV).

I now had a different perspective on the situation. I knew I was in warfare, but did not understand exactly what to make of it. The Lord was outlining what would happen.

The next day, I made a call to a random lawyer in the USA to find out if I had a case and what my rights were as the deceased's wife. I eventually decided not to engage the lawyer and move on with my life. I was alright before him, and I will be alright after him. Besides, the Lord did not tell me to get a lawyer.

I thought about not having a job, my meager savings in the bank, and how I was going to manage. I was unsure if the Lord wanted me to stop working, so I sought Him about it. He sent confirmation that my time at my previous place of employment was up, and He needed me to trust Him.

Wow! No job. Little money. Bills to be paid. Yes, Lord. I will have to trust You.

Honestly, I was nervous because I had never been in that position before.

CHAPTER 7

It was mid-February 2022 when one of my church sisters called me and said she believed the Lord gave her a word for me, so I met with her. She told me that the Lord said I should fight, because He did not bring me to this for nothing. She also said, *"Sis, I feel that this is huge."* She was not the first person to tell me that it was not a simple situation and that there was something big behind it.

The Lord gave me these scriptures:

> *Jeremiah 15:20 – "I will make you a wall to this people, a fortified wall of bronze; they will fight against you but will not overcome you, for I am with you to rescue and save you," declares the LORD. (NIV).*

> *Jeremiah 20:11 - But the LORD is with me like a mighty warrior; so my persecutors will stumble and not prevail. They will fail and be thoroughly disgraced; their dishonor will never be forgotten. (NIV).*

Ruth 4:14 - The women said to Naomi: "Praise be to the LORD, who this day has not left you without a guardian-redeemer. May he become famous throughout Israel!" (NIV).

Please take note of the scriptures; they were very revealing and instructive to me. God is with me; He has not left me an inch.

Then the thought occurred to me to visit my church sister, who is a lawyer. I had noticed that she was quite friendly with me during my months of grief. I approached her and asked her to recommend a lawyer who practices in the U.S. She did, and I had a Zoom meeting with him. He was not impressed with how the daughter handled the situation. He empathized with me.

He took the case and said that he would investigate the properties my husband owned and determine the necessary actions to be taken on the matter. *Thank You, Jesus.* Another positive step had been taken with His help.

In the last week of February, my church began a 21-day fast. Based on the warfare I found myself in, for the first time in my whole Christian life, I committed to such a fast. During the fasting period, only natural food was to be consumed: no white rice and no foods with preservatives. Somehow, I thought it also meant no salt, so I eliminated salt as well. Later on, I found out that we could have salt; however, I decided not to have any for three days. My neighbor, Sonia, suggested that I continue the salt-free diet because of the magnitude of the warfare I was in. The greater the battle, the greater the sacrifice. This was not going to be easy, but I really needed victory over the matter.

The scriptures and sermons I received proved that the Lord was fighting on my behalf, and He was also teaching my hands to war and my fingers to fight.

***Psalm 144:1 - Praise be to the L*ORD** *my Rock, who trains my hands for war, my fingers for battle. (NIV).*

The warfare was intense. Every night from 11:00 pm to 1:00 am, I prayed and read a prayer from Cindy Trimm's book, "**The Rules of Engagement**." She used scriptures to support the prayer points. The book was introduced to me by Sonia.

The Lord had also placed persons who were very strong in warfare prayer in my life. The Lord instructed that they were not to engage in warfare for me, but rather to support me in it. I was so happy that God had used these people to really defend me.

Before I spoke to the lawyer in the U.S., Sandy called me and prayed for me. Many things regarding my situation were revealed to her. She saw my husband's relatives running from the altars that they had set up against me. I was shocked; I could not believe that these people would go to such lengths to get rid of me.

The youngest of my prayer warrior friends told me that I needed to pull down the altars that were set up. Once all those were pulled down, I then needed to set up righteous altars to fight against what was set in motion in the realm of the spirit.

With that instruction, and of course, the "Rules of Engagement" prayers, I took the warfare prayers to a higher level, which included planting financial seeds.

The very first night of my warfare, as I prayed, I saw an altar with my name, shadows of persons, and some unidentifiable items. The power of the Holy Spirit came upon me, and I began to pray in tongues. I noticed that the shadows fled. For about an hour, my hands were doing the pulling and uprooting motions as I sent fire to the persons who had set up the altars.

When I had finished pulling down the altars, I raised up my righteous altars. I began to declare: **"I will not die but live to declare the word of my God."**

The devil was determined. He would take a break, but he would return. He came back, and he continued to come, not through those persons but through others and situations. Once you decide to follow Christ, the devil is upset because he knows the calling on your life. I have the calling of intercession, and I must confess that, through the years, I have not been faithful to the call. These situations drew me right back to my calling and even took me to a higher level.

The plan that these people had with the devil was for me to die, because they thought I married him for his money. I did not know if he had a lot of money, and up until now, I do not know what money they are referring to. They are his family, so they knew more than I. I was still waiting for the Lord to reveal what they knew. What I did know was that he lived on a reasonably sized property.

CHAPTER 8

The warfare took on many forms. The lawyer took the case in February. After countless calls and emails to him went unanswered, I eventually heard from him in May. The lawyer had experienced some family challenges, which included the death of his father-in-law, the hospitalization of his wife, and he too had some health issues. This was warfare at its highest. He told me to try to get in touch with the daughter. I tried, but got no response. We had a Zoom meeting, and based on his findings, there was not a lot of money to be shared, and some had to be paid to a third party. He informed me that the case was outside his jurisdiction. I said, *"Lord, what is this?"* I felt so discouraged. *"Lord, why did You take me to this point to disappoint me?"*

He recommended another lawyer and gave me her contact information. I had the number for a day or two before I decided to send her a WhatsApp text message. In our first conversation, she asked me to call the daughter or send her an email and see if she would respond. I did, and of course, like every other time, she did not respond. The lawyer wrote her a letter, as she could not reach her by phone.

The lawyer wanted to ensure that the daughter was aware that I was her father's wife, and she needed any form of evidence I had. Indeed, I had evidence of our conversations via WhatsApp and email. I had sent the messages along with pictures of my husband lying in the hospital bed to my email for safekeeping because somehow I knew that I would need them.

Remember, his daughter had omitted my name from the death certificate. The lawyer could apply for an amendment; however, his daughter's signature would still be required. The lawyer requested copies of my ID, marriage certificate, and the death certificate.

CHAPTER 9

Sonia, whom the Lord had chosen to give me guidance, said we needed to take the matter to the courtroom of heaven, which we did. The Lord said this case is to be tried. I felt relieved and thankful to the Lord.

The term "Courtroom of Heaven" is actually another level in the strategy of warfare when the devil brings charges against you, and God, the presiding Judge, hears your case and makes a judgment as to whether you are guilty or not. It is set up similarly to our courts here on earth. Here are a few scriptures about it for your reading, and there are others you can research:

Psalm 82:1-8 - God presides in the great assembly; he renders judgment among the "gods": "How long will you defend the unjust and show partiality to the wicked? Defend the weak and the fatherless; uphold the cause of the poor and the oppressed. Rescue the weak and the needy; deliver them from the hand of the wicked. "The 'gods' know nothing, they understand nothing. They walk about in darkness; all the foundations of the earth are shaken. "I said, 'You are "gods"; you are all sons of the Most High.' But you will die like mere mortals; you will fall like every other ruler." Rise up, O God, judge the earth, for all the nations are your inheritance. (NIV).

Daniel 7:9-10 - As I looked, "thrones were set in place, and the Ancient of Days took his seat. His clothing was as white as snow; the hair of his head was white like wool. His throne was flaming with fire, and its wheels were all ablaze. A river of fire was flowing, coming out from before him. Thousands upon thousands attended him; ten thousand times ten thousand stood before him. The court was seated, and the books were opened." (NIV).

One night, I had a dream. My deceased husband was standing next door. He was holding an envelope, and he said, *"I have been looking for you to give you this envelope. I couldn't find you, but I'm happy I found you because I want you to have this."* I took it and looked inside; it contained some documents and money. I told him I had prayed to the Lord for him not to find me because he was dead. The dream ended.

CHAPTER 10

The lawyer told me that she had written a very stern letter to his daughter, to which she had responded. Later, she told me that the daughter had called her office and stated that she was not aware that her father had a wife. *Wow!* She had no idea that I could stay in Jamaica and take action. The lawyer informed me that his daughter had already taken steps to sell the property, but the judge had denied her the right to do so. My lawyer did not understand why she was denied the right to sell, but I knew that my God was at work. She even tried to get her brother to lose interest in the property, so she would be the sole inheritor, but little did she know that God in heaven is a God of justice.

The case was in the judge's hands, but my God was the presiding Judge.

The battle continued. The daughter and her aunt constantly went to places of evil to try to kill me. When that did not work, they tried to drive me out of my mind, and at one point even tried to cripple my body. Evil spirits would enter my room, and I could not move or call out to anyone. Medically, it is called sleep paralysis, but it is not a physical phenomenon; it is a spiritual one. Let no one tell you that it is a paralysis; it is evil, and it is a spiritual attack. The warfare had intensified because I dared to seek a lawyer to get what I rightfully deserved.

While still under the spiritual attacks, I remembered that the Lord reads our minds. Immediately, I thought, *"Lord, please send angelic assistance now."* And true to my request, I was able to get up. I was mad in the spirit, so I read some scriptures about warfare. I walked through the house, praying and repeating:

> ***Luke 10:19 - I have given you authority to trample on snakes and scorpions and to overcome all the power of the enemy; nothing will harm you. (NIV).***
>
> ***Isaiah 54:17 – "no weapon forged against you will prevail, and you will refute every tongue that accuses you. This is the heritage of the servants of the LORD, and this is their vindication from me." (NIV).***

Psalm 127:2b - for he grants sleep to those he loves. (NIV).

Hence, I must sleep in peace; therefore, I went back to sleep.

Over a couple of months, the attacks came in many ways, such as memory loss, confusion, and lightheadedness. *Lord, what is this?* My physical body was weak, and I wondered if I needed iron supplements.

I went to church, and a brother told me that the Lord had revealed to him that some people were trying to drive me crazy. He prayed for my mind. Keep in mind that this brother was unaware of my entanglement with my in-laws.

At home, during my nightly prayers, I uttered, *"Oh, so a mad you a try mad me? Okay, back to sender with the blood of Jesus!"* I blasted in tongues. For those who do not believe in speaking in tongues, read:

1 Corinthians 14:2-4 - For anyone who speaks in a tongue does not speak to people but to God. Indeed, no one understands them; they utter mysteries by the Spirit. But

the one who prophesies speaks to people for their strengthening, encouraging and comfort. Anyone who speaks in a tongue edifies themselves, but the one who prophesies edifies the church. (NIV).

Speaking in tongues gives you the capacity to war because you may not have the right words to say. The Lord also downloads things to you during this time.

I went to sleep and dreamt that his family was quarreling among themselves. They were asking his sister why she used such strong medicine on him. *Did you just read what I said?* This was extremely revealing, showing the extent to which a person will go to get their way.

During these times, I had many dreams in which I fought dogs, tore open their jawbones, and retrieved keys from the owner of the dogs, who eventually turned into a dog. I dreamt of people giving me keys on different occasions. The dreams signified victory and access.

I later learnt that when it was proven that she had lied about being unaware of her father's marriage, her lawyer was not pleased with her and, at one point, wanted to drop her case.

Battle for Another Level

My lawyer filed the necessary paperwork to get my name added to the death certificate, but his daughter tried to block it every step of the way so I would not get any portion of the property.

The battles in my dream were relentless, which included frogs. I would kill them, but they would return. I asked the Lord what was happening, and He reminded me of David and Goliath—that David killed Goliath with a stone and then beheaded him. This meant that I was not only to kill the frogs, but also to burn them, which I did, and that was the end of that form of attack.

The lawyer would tell me how the daughter continued to frustrate the process, and at times, she would not speak to her lawyer or mine.

There were times I wanted to give up; my strength was well spent. Sonia prayed for my strength and encouraged me; I also called out to God for myself. The Lord said:

Jeremiah 12:5 - "If you have raced with men on foot and they have worn you out, how can you compete with horses? If you stumble in safe country, how will you

manage in the thickets by the Jordan?" *(NIV).*

I had to pray for myself because I was the one in training; the time would come when I would have to do battle for others.

CHAPTER 11

Apart from the spiritual challenges, I also faced financial challenges, but I could not ask for help because the Lord told me not to ask anyone for anything, as He is my source, and He would not have me begging for bread. He said I should stand still and see the salvation of the Lord. That is easier said than done.

I had a wedding to attend. At first, I decided to wear an outfit from my closet. A church sister was selling some clothes she received from overseas, so I credited a dress, and we agreed on a payment date. However, she disregarded our agreement and requested a portion of the payment. The Lord rebuked me and said, *"Didn't I tell you that I am your source? What you don't understand is that people are saying all kinds of things about you. They don't know your situation. Take the dress back."* I felt bad, but I said, *"Lord, I have to take what was said about me because I shouldn't have credited it."* I cannot tell you how many times I repented and begged God not to punish me for disobedience.

You know what the Lord did? As I searched my closet for an outfit, someone called me and asked what I was doing. I explained what I was doing, and she asked when the wedding would be. A few days later, she called and told me to go to Kingston to collect a package. The package had everything I needed for the wedding. With that, I learned my lesson.

There were so many occasions when the Lord showed up right on time. One particular Sunday at church, I sat with my head down, thinking about the servicing of my car, when a sister came and stood before me and said, *"Haven't I taken care of you? Why are you worried? I will never leave you."* I immediately knew that it was the Lord speaking.

CHAPTER 12

Proverbs 21:15 - When justice is done, it brings joy to the righteous but terror to evildoers. (NIV).

It's August 2023.

Yes, courts sometimes take a long time to deal with matters, but throughout this time, I kept my prayer watch, praying and fasting twice a week, and also gave sacrificial offerings. The lawyer called to say that the court had acknowledged me as the deceased's spouse, and the death certificate was amended to reflect that.

Thank You, Jesus!

Earlier in the month, I had a dream in which documents were being signed. Then came the praise stopper: the daughter took the matter to another court, trying to stop me from getting what the Lord had told me to fight for. The months passed, and in 2024, the battle is still ongoing.

Her lawyer dropped the case, but thank God, he was not needed at that point. She was mad that the court ruled in my favour. Although I was in a foreign country, I was entitled to my husband's share of the property. The witchcraft continued!

One morning, I woke up with my back and legs in pain; I could hardly stand. I iced the areas to relieve the pain, but it didn't work, so I said, *"What now, Lord?"* I rebuked it and used epsom salt in warm water; glory to God, I was delivered.

Isaiah 54:17 – "no weapon forged against you will prevail, and you will refute every tongue that accuses you. This is the heritage of the servants of the LORD, and this is their indication from me," declares the LORD. (NIV).

This has been my anthem, and indeed, God is faithful to perform His Word.

I received the documents from the lawyer in 2025, on the last day of my three-day fast. They came in a white envelope just as I had dreamt. I know this may shock some people, but I have no idea what God's appointed lawyer looks like. Yes, the lawyer who worked the case here on earth. We had planned to

FaceTime at the end of the case, but it didn't materialize.

This experience and training taught me that it's about God. Whenever she called or if I called her, I felt an inner peace. The devil did make suggestions, and my response was, *"It is not my case, it's the Lord's, and she doesn't work with me."* I am God's steward and mouthpiece.

The battle with the daughter did not end in the realm of the spirit. The Lord told me to go on a three-day fast to destroy the newly sent blows, which I did. There are still attempts being made because the real enemy is Satan, and he is a stubborn being; therefore, as Christians, we have to stay in the secret place, and God will give us the strategy for the season. In each battle we face with Satan, there is a strategy that the Lord must manifest to bring about the victory that is ours.

I am truly grateful and give God all the praise for guiding me through this battle. It has allowed me to grow in Christ because I have seen and learned new things about the enemy, but more importantly, about my all-powerful God.

Whenever I felt like I couldn't make it because it was too hard, I told myself that there are some things that the enemy will not allow some of us to have, so we must persevere and never give up. Satan's agents do not sleep; they constantly service their altars. Why shouldn't I do the same, knowing that I serve an all-powerful King of all kings, Jehovah Gibbor?

I have grown spiritually because I have learned, and I am still learning, about God, and I will never stop learning. The sooner we accept the Word of God, which teaches that we are in constant warfare, the sooner we realize that the battles are already won. When we do our part to manifest that victory, it will be better for us.

It is my prayer that this testimony will be of great help to persons who are presently fighting the battle of their lives. God is training you.

> ***Psalm 144:1-2 - Praise be to the Lord my Rock, who trains my hands for war, my fingers for battle. He is my loving God and my fortress, my stronghold and my deliverer, my shield, in whom I take refuge, who subdues peoples under me. (NIV).***

We are soldiers, not civilians!

My prayers are with you, dear reader.

God bless you.

ABOUT THE AUTHOR

Paula Marie Stewart relocated to the vibrant parish of St. Catherine, Jamaica in her late teens. She is a devoted Christian, a passionate educator, and a visionary entrepreneur whose life has been marked by a strong faith and a purposeful service.

With over thirty years of steadfast Christian Walk, Paula holds the title of the longest-standing member in her local church, known for her deep love for the Lord and her commitment to the things of God. Her faith is not just personal—it is a lifestyle that has shaped every role she has embraced.

As a **Sunday school teacher**, Paula has sown seeds of biblical truth into the hearts of children, nurturing their spiritual growth and guiding them to know and love God. Her work as an **early childhood educator** reflects her passion for laying strong foundations in the lives of the youngest learners. Through her nurturing spirit and dedication, she has impacted countless young lives, both spiritually and academically.

Paula is also a **lay preacher**, faithfully sharing the Word of God with boldness, clarity, and passion. Her messages are known to inspire transformation and encourage deeper walks with Christ.

In addition to her ministry work, Paula is a driven **entrepreneur.** Her business pursuits reflect her integrity, creativity, and a strong sense of purpose rooted in her faith.

Throughout her life, Paula Marie Stewart has embodied what it means to live for Christ. Whether in the classroom, church, or marketplace, she carries a heart of service and a deep desire to see God's will done on earth. She continues to be a beacon of light, a source of wisdom, and a faithful servant of the Lord.

www.ingramcontent.com/pod-product-compliance
Lightning Source LLC
Chambersburg PA
CBHW071316110426
42743CB00042B/2589